T0380858

A FABULOUS MODEL "T" ADVENTURE

By Charles and Kenneth Whitsett
Orland, California

Print information available on the last page

Rev. date: 04/12/2019

To order additional copies of this book, contact:
Xlibris
1-888-795-4274
www.Xlibris.com
Orders@Xlibris.com

Beginning of the Ford Model T Story
Ken needed transportation

Ken sold his 1937 Ford car to take flying lessons during his high school junior year (1946). He played football at Orland High School and the practice lasted until 5 o'clock and began again after 7:30 pm, so Ken needed some transportation. He rode his bicycle for a while, but this method was not satisfactory since he lived 5 miles from town.

Homer Ellsworth, the High School shop teacher told Ken and his friend, Lloyd Schaffert, that their shop project could be restoring a Ford Model T. They learned how to set up the milling machine to mill .050 inch off the engine head, weld the fender cracks, clean the ring grooves and pistons and adjust the bearings. They adapted 1942 Ford wheels to replace the old wooden spoke wheels so they could use the popular 6.00/16 tires. They gave the car a good overhaul.

Ken's father, Willis Whitsett had a textbook, "Dykes Handbook for Automotive Engineering", that the boys could study and follow directions. Finally, his mechanical transportation problems were solved!

Ken at Highschool

Then Ken painted the car with yellow paint left over from painting the John Deere tractor.

A few times Ken found his Model T between two trees or on the lawn in front of the principal's office–just kids playing tricks on Ken.

Model T History

One day, in 1946 Ken had spotted an old 1924 Model T Roadster next to a neighbor, Fred Canadas's barn and he inquired about buying it. Ken gave him the $10 he was asking for the Model T. He found that one of the wheel bearings was missing when he got the car home. He went back to see if he could find the bearing. Fred gave him 50 cents and said to go buy a new bearing. Ken's first "Model T" cost $9.50. This is the car that Ken and his friend worked on in the high school shop.

The next was a 1919 Model T and it was free. Another neighbor, Harry Goettsch, had bought a new Model T touring car soon after the WWI and used it until 1928 when he parked it. When Ken went over and asked him about it, he gave it to him. Ken dragged it home with the John Deere tractor and parked it near the barn. Every time he went out to milk the cows, he would kick the crank to see if he could turn the crankshaft but it wouldn't budge. The spark plugs were left out and the hood was gone, so rain had filled the cylinders with water for years. He drained the water out and poured tractor fuel in the sparkplug holes and kept trying. One day the crank moved a little.

In time he could turn the crankshaft by hand. (Note) This 1919 engine turned out to be the one that was used for most of the cross-country trip and for a year after at college.

Ken bought the third Model T, which he had located about 5 miles south of Orland next to Walker Creek for $25.00. This Model T was a 1926 coupe with wire wheels and roll-up windows and had the engine that was expected to be used on the cross-country trip.

Ken took the engine to a local machine shop, in the spring of 1947, to have it overhauled and new bearings poured. The shop sent the engine to Sacramento to have this specialty work done.

Ken and Charlie had to decide whether to select the closed cab coupe or the open roadster to fix up for the trip. Since the roadster was sportier and painted yellow, it was chosen.

Ken kept asking about the status of the engine project – with no satisfaction. By early June, just after graduation, it became apparent alternate plans for a "T" engine had to be made. (Note) The local machine shop contacted Ken after the trip was over and said, "Your engine is ready", Ken said, "Keep the engine, we already took our trip". They wanted $150. A few months later the shop agreed to let him have it for $75 and he picked it up.

The fourth and final Model T came from a farmer between the Sacramento River and State Route 45. The farmer had a 1924 Model T but he said, "You can have the engine and parts", but he wanted the car frame for gateposts.

This is the engine that was used as a spare for the cross-country trip. Charlie welded an angle iron stand to stabilize the engine on behind the cab. Ken found a Model T trailer hitch and installed it on the rear spring u-bolts.

Testing the First Engine

The county had recently cut a road down a hill to connect to Hwy 32 east of Orland.

Ken and Charlie found out what happens when you over—rev the engine. They were not use to the gas control on the steering column instead of on the floor.

The down hill (over revved) engine caused a broken crankshaft.

They walked home and pulled the disabled car home and learned a valuable lesson they never forgot. This was the Model T Ken got for $9 50.

NOTES: **Events and earning funds in preparation for the cross country trip**

- Re-leveled farm fields
- Worked fields and irrigated with new dykes
- Planted corn for silage
- Trip took place while the corn was growing
- Frank Manner chopped the corn and filled the silo
- Added a 1928 Chevrolet transmission behind the T transmission, this gave more power for the hills.
- Had the cloth top and seats reupholstered
- Charlie purchased a new Kit Camper trailer
- Added a full length wooden tool box on the passenger side running board and filled it with spare parts and tools, including a 1-½ ton chain hoist

Our Model T trip from California to New York and Back

On Aug. 1st, 1947, we began our trip from Orland, California along the highway through Oroville. We stopped to let the engine cool off on this steep grade and saw a 5-gallon can that had been lost from a passing vehicle. It was full of gasoline. This helped us climb out of the Feather River Canyon on our way to our first stop near Reno, Nevada. Since we had a big day getting ready and a slow trip through the mountains we were ready to try out the Kit Camper trailer for a good night's sleep. We did not realize where we were in this high desert land. Early in the morning the airplanes flying low over our heads startled us. We had no idea that we were at the end of the runway of the Reno airport!

As we left the Reno area and headed toward Salt Lake City we chased jackrabbits and saw pronghorn antelopes in the distance. Our first mechanical problem happened when some young fellows heading for Florida from Reno, ran into the back of our Kit Camper/trailer. They were not paying attention to their speed nor our slow speed. They admitted it was their fault and wrote us a check on a Florida Bank for $25.00 and they drove away. We were left to fix what we could before moving on. The ball hitch was broken on the back of the Model T and the aluminum hinged cover over our kitchen was damaged. Later we found that the check was no good. We had a propane stove, ice box, water supply and food storage in the trailer. Those parts of the trailer were OK. We used a chain, bolts, and bailing wire to bandage our wounds. After repairs, we continued on.

We noticed a large (junk area) collection of old Model Ts near Battle Mountain, Nevada. This might come in handy for repairs if needed.

In Wyoming we stopped at a gas station/store and asked when we would get out of this desert? The attendant said, "This is no desert, it is a high plateau".

The "T" was modified with a 1928 Chevrolet transmission that allowed us to climb in a lower gear, or use a low gear in going down a steep grade. Our lowest gear was double reverse (the Chevrolet transmission in reverse and Model T reverse pedal). We found a way to keep the Chevrolet transmission from slipping out of gear by attaching a heavy wire to the dashboard and the gearshift lever; otherwise, we would have to hold the gearshift lever with our hand.

The next significant Chevrolet transmission trouble was near Rollins, Wyoming, 40 miles to the west of where we were stranded.

Ken put a jack under the engine in order to remove the damaged parts.

The front shaft of the Chevrolet transmission had worn round rather than square where it fits into the rear of the Model T transmission. Although he put on his coveralls, it was still a dirty job. He cleaned up using a hubcap with gasoline plus soap and water.

He was ready to put the parts in a flour sack, and became more presentable wearing his school sweater, and then thumbing a ride into Rollins.

Ken was gone more than half a day while Charlie stayed with the car inside the camper trailer. Charlie wrote letters to parents, sister, girl friends and relatives that had not heard from us since we left home.

The 80-mile trip for Ken to Rollins and back was successful except for the transmission ball cap that was left on the workbench at the repair shop.

Ken had to hitchhike all the way back and get it before the assembly could take place.

Charlie fixed a nice meal and had it ready when he returned. We were both tired and waited until morning to work on the car again.

Ken Under the "T"

Ken Taking Things Apart for Repairs

When all was back in place we proceeded on east.

The front connecting rod began to make a disturbing knock as we ventured up a long hill into Nebraska. We stopped near a grove of trees (for shade) just off the road and decided to troubleshoot the problem. We drained the oil into a can, removed the pan, and found the worn rod. We drained the radiator, took off the head and removed the piston and rod that was involved. We carried a few spare parts in our toolbox that covered the running board on the passenger side of the car. We replaced the worn rod and removed brass shims until it fit with a little drag on the crankshaft. We were ready to put back the parts needed; the pan, head, oil, and water for the radiator. This repair took us all day. Our supper was a can of peaches, and we called it a day.

We saw signs like "Cozad, Nebraska, The Alfalfa Capital of the World". The beautiful rolling hills with cornfields were everywhere as far as we could see. This was truly spectacular compared to the 60-70 acres of corn we left back home.

The only time we went around (passed) a vehicle on our trip was when we were near the highest point of the Rocky Mountains.

Top of the Grade

A heavily loaded P.I.E. truck was in a low gear and the driver motioned us to go around him as he pulled over, giving us more room to avoid any on-coming cars. With our very modest, sporty Ford Model T & trailer, we inched our way around successfully.

This was on the Lincoln Hwy 30, which then was a two-lane road. Now it is Interstate 80 Freeway.

The people in the Midwest (Iowa/Indiana) treated us with big smiles, waves and special attention.

The first stop was Monticello, Indiana, where we spent about a week with our relatives. It was relaxing to visit. We were fed big farm type meals, rested, avoided doing dishes, and having to find food to eat.

On the day we arrived, we telephoned home and talked to our folks and told them some of our activities and got caught up on some of the back home news.

The relatives were happy to show us around the local area. One day they said "would you like an airplane ride to view the Tippecanoe River and farms?" We said, "that would be great!" They arranged a ticket for Charlie, but Ken said he was a student pilot and wanted to go up and fly himself. They had him practice a few trips around the pattern and he was ready to go alone. This was a very special day.

Our relatives included grandmother's cousin, Margarite, and Bob Zootman, her husband. They lived in Orland in the late 20's and early 30's. Their son, Max, and daughter, Ina Marie were young teenagers when we saw last them.

Bob was a blacksmith, mechanic and a machinist in his prime years. When Bob and his wife came to visit in Orland in 1946, Bob had nearly lost his eyesight, but he was a great help in solving Model T problems for Ken. Bob diagnosed ignition and carburetor problems by the sound and vibrations.

During our visit we took pictures of Bob in the yellow Model T on his farm. We were gathered for dinner with many cousins we had never heard of, but they enjoyed the stories of our trip.

The fence posts at their farm had marks caused by hail stones the size of golf balls. The ears of corn were in storage sheds with wire sides for air circulation.

The frost kills the corn stalks and leaves before harvest—some times they wait until the ground is frozen and snow is on the ground before they harvest.

After family group pictures were taken, and boxes of food were packed, we were ready to head north toward Michigan. Leaving Monticello we saw a beautiful old barn. It was nearly 100 years old and looked like new. It had a slate roof and rock walls. We had to take a picture of this unusual site.

Old Slate Roof Barn

We came to a town named "Orland, Indiana, population 307". We just had to get a picture of that also.

Orland, Indiana

We arrived in Detroit and thought about going to the Ford Plant, but got on Michigan Avenue. The posted signs said "No Right Turn" and "No Left Turn" and "Tunnel to Canada", so we had no choice but to follow this route. We decided we would come through Detroit on our way back from New York.

It was a cloudy day and fog was thick along Lake Erie. We were stopped at a check station as we left USA and entered Canada. They asked us several questions, such as "Do you have any firearms"? "Yes, a 22 rifle". "What is under the canvas behind the cab? "A spare engine, we said". They told us "you are not permitted to bring these kinds of things across the border". We explained that we needed spare parts if anything needed to be replaced. They sealed the .22 rifle barrel and said they would inspect it upon our return. Finally they let us continue toward Niagara Falls and the Buffalo area.

After a while the fog lifted and we noticed rows of green leafy plants that turned out to be tobacco.

Field of Tobacco

Near Wellandport, Canada, we began to have some engine problems.

The miss-firing cylinder could be a big problem. We checked the spark plug, wiring, the commutator and coil, but could not find the problem. The engine had gotten pretty hot earlier so we thought that might have caused the problem.

While we were stopped along a country road, a farmer and his two boys were coming with a team of horses pulling a load of loose hay. Since it looked like rain, they were anxious to haul in feed for their livestock. The farmer suggested that we pull the car and trailer to his house and we could work on the car in his barn because he knew there was a big storm coming.

We left the trailer by the house and pushed the car into a large old barn. This Hungarian family named (Sefranos) insisted that we eat with them.

We told them we would sleep in our own bed in the trailer but we did enjoy their hospitality and food.

The next day we used our chain hoist attached to one of the large log poles supporting the hayloft.

With the hoist we pulled the engine out and made preparations to assemble the accessories on the spare engine.

A large thunderstorm came through with lightning and a real downpour of rain and hail. The lightning rod on the barn caused static electricity to bite us when we began working on the car. The bolt of lightning killed two horses in the neighbor's field that night.

It took us three days to complete the engine exchange before we would head to Niagara Falls. We thanked the Sefranos family for all they did for us and tested our workmanship again. The engine seemed to run well.

Niagara Falls was fantastic! We crossed the Rainbow Bridge and parked for a while and saw the party boat *Maid of the Mist* in the pool of water at the base of the falls.

Niagara Falls

Rainbow Bridge from Canada

We could not afford the luxury of the boat trip so we settled for a milk shake. Charlie ordered a strawberry and Ken a marshmallow shake. The waitress asked if we wanted a malt? Ken described to the young gal how to make the special shake without malt and when she used too much of the marshmallow flavor, she got in trouble with her boss. The shakes were a real treat!

We went south for about 20-25 miles to Buffalo, New York and decided not to continue east. The spare engine was using more oil than it should and we needed to be home for college to start on September 5th.

We decided to head back to the border crossing and through the tunnel to Detroit. Getting back to the USA was OK and they checked to see if the .22 rifle was still sealed.

On our way back into Detroit we stopped a few times to ask for directions to the Ford Motor Company plant. We finally found a security guard at one of the entrances.

He advised us to go to a specific entrance near the Ford Rotunda building about 9:00 a.m. the next morning.

We found a side street near a large highway ramp (overpass that crossed a river) and this is where we parked overnight and did some cleaning. We both worked hard cleaning the dirt and mud from the trailer and oil and grease from the T. After all, this was a homecoming for the Model T and we wanted everything to look good.

We dressed up in slacks, sport shirts and jackets and then drove to the special entrance. The guard called to announce our arrival and we were met with a guest-relations executive in front of the Ford Rotunda Building.

In Front of the Ford Rotunda

Ford's PR-Man at the Wheel

Ken and Charlie at the Ford Rotunda

The Day at the Ford plant

Our personal guide called a photographer from the advertising department to come and take pictures of our visit. Many executives parked their fancy limousines in front of this building and they all had to move them. They made us feel special.

After pictures we were directed to a parking lot and then taken on a tour of the entire Ford plant and related areas.

The guide showed us the plant where they stamped out the metal for the fenders, doors and hoods of the new models not yet seen in showrooms. It was very interesting to see the test track where the new cars were studied for performance.

On our way past the Henry Ford's burial plot monument, we could see ships loaded with steel and other raw materials for the plant.

The assembly was done in large buildings with many workers. It was interesting to see a large roll of steel pulled out over a press and then with a loud "crunch", there was a new fender.

The next event was the Dearborn Inn, a very exclusive restaurant. Our guide went to the hat/coat check stand and got neckties for us so we could enter for lunch. We were given the royal treatment as special guests that day. There was much to see in the Henry Ford Museum and we could hardly manage in the time frame we had. Our guest executive sent us four (8"x 10") photos of this event as he had promised. The pictures were published in a Ford magazine and in the newspaper in Windsor, Canada. These two farm boys will never forget this experience.

Engine change Again

Leaving Detroit, we went west for 50 miles or more then northwest to the Lansing, Michigan area. The same problem we had in Rollins, Nebraska happened again. The transmission shaft had worn round like before. In Fowlerville, Michigan, we found a small one-man auto repair shop that was willing to help us fix the problem with the transmission shaft. We decided to change back to the 1919 engine since the spare engine was burning so much oil.

After checking the old engine and finding it to be sound, we made the necessary repairs. This time we drilled a hole through the Chevrolet transmission shaft and welded in a piece of 3/8 inch drill bit and cut slots in the mating surface on the rear of the T transmission.

We then repaired the 1919 engine by lapping the valves and tightening the bearings.

We had to file the bearing caps to take out the play between the crankshaft and the rod bearing. Each piston rod was tightened to the crankshaft as well as the main bearings and when all was back together the crank used to turn the engine would not budge. The owner of the shop connected his tow truck to a chain around the front axel and pulled our Ford with a jerk and bent the front axle. He used his acetylene torch and heated the axle to a cherry red color and used a sledgehammer to bend it straight. This time we used the crank and starter at the same time and got the engine started. While waiting at a stoplight in downtown Lansing, the engine died. Ken was cranking by hand and Charlie was using the foot starter button. Finally it began to run again.

People in the lanes on each side of us stopped and they began honking and commenting on our predicament. Leaving Lansing with its congested traffic and our embarrassing troubles, we headed north to Mackinaw City to catch a short ferry ride to Sault Ste Marie.

Mackinaw Ferry Ride

We then drove along the south edge of Lake Superior to Duluth, Minnesota.

We were on our way and made good time, each driving about 6-8 hours per day, stopping only for food, gas and restrooms.

In North Dakota we stopped one night and got in the trailer to sleep. Even with our clothes on and all the blankets, it was too cold to sleep. So we drove all night enjoying the heat from the exhaust pipe through a hole in the floorboards and tucking blankets on both sides of the convertible top to keep out the wind.

On this northern route, some places only sold bread that was frozen; a new experience for us. They had very little business in this remote area.

While in Montana, we heard a sound that we thought was a main bearing knocking. We found a suitable railroad bridge where we could use our chain hoist to lift up the front end of the Ford. This made it easier to tighten the main and rod bearings. This time we were careful not to get the bearings too tight to turn the crank.

We saw an old Holt steel wheeled steam tractor across the drain ditch that looked interesting, but was of no use to us. When all was fixed we used both transmissions in reverse for the lowest gear forward to get us back up the steep bank on to the roadway.

Glacier National Park

We enjoyed the trip through this "high plateau", and especially the Glacier National Park's "Going to the Sun Highway". This is a very steep and winding roadway

With our seven forward speeds chugging along up this grade of 10% or more, we made it just fine. The view of the mountains and glacier was spectacular. The Park will allow only vehicles up to 21 feet long because of the sharp switchbacks. We stopped at a beautiful lake on the west side of the park and tried fishing for an hour or two without any luck. Later at a store we asked about the fishing at that lake, and they told us "No one ever gets any fish out of that lake".

Then we went on through Idaho and on to Pasco, Washington where the universal joint came apart. Ken removed the universal joint and hitchhiked into town to get new rivets installed to hold the universal joint together.

After putting things back in place, we went on across the Columbia River and drove day and night through Oregon and Northern California.

Some of the most beautiful snow-covered mountains came into view through Oregon and northern California. The view of Mount Shasta at about 5:30 in the morning was a beautiful and welcomed sight.

Mount Schasta

We were able to keep up with a greyhound bus on a steep downhill grade on the way to Redding, California. We were getting anxious to get home and this familiar landscape in the Northern Sacramento valley made us act like a horse heading for the barn. We arrived back home in Orland on a Friday September 2nd to the open arms of our Mom and Dad.

On Monday September 5th we had to register for college at Grant Technical College in North Sacramento (now American River College). We had traveled about 6,500 miles and, yes we had troubles but it all was worth it.

This was the conclusion of the longest trip we ever made in the Model T, but many shorter ones followed during our college days. We drove about 100 miles from Sacramento each time we came home to Orland for a weekend. Other field trips and vacation trips were a little longer.

On a trip to San Francisco on a class outing we had a valve top break off and punched a hole in the piston. We had a spare valve but not a spare piston. We took the piston out and hiked into San Rafael and found a blacksmith shop. The blacksmith welded a metal patch over the hole in the cast iron piston. When it had cooled off, we hiked back and installed the piston and valve and went on our way.

Another field trip took us to Stinson Beach and on the way home we went up Highway 101 through the Redwoods. There was a little snow on the ground and on the trees. Charlie and Ken had a classmate, Glenn Zimmerman with us on this trip.

College Trip – See the Trailer Damage

On the way from Eureka to Redding we ran low on gas while going up a long hill near Douglas City. Glenn and Ken hiked back to a small town and got a gallon of gas while Charlie waited by the camper and Model T. It was after dark but we had moonlight. We poured the gas in the tank and found that the hill was still too steep for the gravity feed to the carburetor. In the old days we heard you could back up a hill when the gas was too low but we couldn't do it with the camper attached. We scratched our heads a little and decided to use the tire pump to add pressure in the gas tank to force the gas to feed to the carburetor. With the seat out, Glenn and Charlie pumped air through the little vent hole in the gas cap and Ken started the engine. Ken stood out on the running board while steering the car and Glenn and Charlie continued pumping until we got to the top of the hill. Down hill was easy then and we drove into Douglas City where we could get gas the next morning.

One day at college, the rear end gear broke. Ken borrowed a car that evening and drove home to Orland where he had more gears. The next day after classes, he changed out the bad gear. Later we were going to the store for food but the car went backward in forward gears and forward in the back up gear. Ken had reversed the ring and pinion gear. So we went to the store using reverse. The next day Ken corrected the problem.

When the freshman year was over, Ken installed the engine he had the machine shop rebuild. It was the 1926 engine that didn't get ready in time for the long trip. In a few hundred miles a rod bearing burned out. Ken found out later that the rebabbitt job was done poorly. After this the Model T wasn't used again and was dismantled in 1954 . . .

Restoration of the 1924 Ford Model T Begins

In 1968 Ken started the restoration of the Model T by sandblasting the frame, fenders and other parts and prime painted them. He rounded up other parts that were needed to bring the car back to original condition including wood spoke wheels. He rebuilt the starter, carburetor, generator, instrument panel, spring perch bushings and differential. Not much more was done until Ken's son Don volunteered to help with putting the Model T back together starting in the fall of 2007. What took so long to start the restoration? Well it didn't help that Ken was moved 8 times by his employer after the Model T was dismantled.

After 60 years since the trip, Ken and Don are restoring the old car.

Henry Ford said, "You can have any color you want as long as it is black"

Ken and Son

So Don is putting the frame and body back together and painting it black.

Frame and Engine Go Together

Ken rebuilt the engine and transmission. He installed .010 oversized rebabbitted connecting rods that were X'ed and drilled top and bottom and with oil dippers. The rear main bearing had too much endplay and this could cause major damage to the magneto coils. So Ken asked Dood Greene of Yuba City, Ca. to add .021 inch of babbitt to take up the endplay.

It was necessary to replace the freeze plugs in the block with new brass ones. He installed a .003-oversized rebabbitted universal ball cap at the rear of the transmission. He also installed new Kevlar band linings.

Don had a new flat tube core installed in the radiator for better cooling.

Don and Ken installed the engine in the frame and installed all new wiring and a new 6 volt battery. A compression test proved at leased 50 pounds compression on all cylinders. The engine was started and ran very nicely.

Don got the wheel rims and hubs ready for George Garrigan's "Vintage Wheel Shop" in Sonora, California to put in new hickory wooden spokes.

Ken took the wheels up to Sonora and picked them up when completed. The drive down the old gold rush highway 49 was spectacular. George finished the job with great looking wheels.

We got the wooden body parts from Cubel's, "Fordwood" shop in Utah. The body wood kit had to be installed before the body metal could be installed.

Some of the body parts had rusted through and left holes. Don used fiberglass to fill the holes and reinforce the thin areas. He welded many tears and cracks in the body parts.

Ken ordered new headlight reflectors and light bulbs and installed these in the newly painted headlight frames. Mike, Charlie's son made new sheet metal parts for the rear and side sills and a new bottom for the original Ford tool box. Mike has his own air-conditioning and sheet metal business.

Ken installed new upholstery for the seat and backrest. He installed new glass in the windshield. Then Don and Ken assembled the fenders, splash panels, running boards and hood.

Now it looks more like it did 85 years ago.

We took several folks for test rides and all worked well. We still have the top to install.

This ends a lot of work and a labor of love now to be enjoyed in parades and short trips.

Wood Body in place–Test drive

Model "T" Almost Finished

Fortunately there are several Companies that have catalogs with most of the Model T parts needed for a quality restoration job. Some of these are: Lang's, Mac's, Snyder's, Chaffin's as well as Sacramento Vintage Ford Parts Inc.

Dood Green of Yuba City, California added babbitt to the rear main bearing to reduce the endplay with the crankshaft.

Milt Webb "The Instructor" of Elk Grove, California, was very helpful by showing us how some parts should be installed and adjusted properly as well as a lot of good advise.

Orland Youths Back From 6,500 Mile Trip In Ancient 1919 Ford

With their faithful old Ford motor of 1919 vintage purring along even better than when they left Orland on Aug.1st, Kenneth and Charles Whitsett, sons of Mr. and Mrs. Willis Whitsett, drove into town Friday night, completing a 33-day tour of the country which covered 6500 miles and dozens of states. The ancient car with its 1924 body, long a familiar sight on the streets of Orland, created no end of comment wherever it chugged along, pulling a sportsmen trailer In which the boys slept. Straight across country they went by way of Salt Lake City, and on to Buffalo, New York and Niagara Falls stopping where and when their fancy and the ancient motor dictated. They created somewhat of a sensation when they chugged into the Ford plant at Dearborn. There they were honored guests of the Ford company for the entire day, and a given a special guide for just the two of them for a tour of the giant plant and the Ford Museum. They had their pictures taken by the official Ford photographer alongside of their ancient model before the rotunda and this will be published in the Ford magazine. The youthful explorers did not venture into traffic jammed New York, but confined all trips in that section to upper state. Homeward they hit Highway 2 and traveled straight across the upper rim of the United States, down to the Columbia, on to Klamath by the Bend highway, and on home by Weed, coasting most of the way from Shasta Dam. Sure the lads had car trouble here and there, but never once did the ancient car have to be driven into a garage for repairs, for the boys took along their own kit of tools and turned roadside spot into an emergency garage. They even carried along an extra motor, a real modern one, vintage 1924, which they installed along the roadside back East, but only used it a thousand miles, as it proved to be an oil eater, and they stopped and put back the old one, getting about 18 miles to a gallon.

The two boys, both graduates of Orland High, Charles, forty-five, and Kenneth in forty-seven, picked up a good share of skill of doctoring Fords while taking shop at the local school. Most of the time on the trip they were on their own, sleeping out where and how they pleased, visiting relatives only once in Indiana. When they left Orland August 1st, a lot of folks predicted that they would not get beyond Reno or at any rate, come back by train when the ancient Ford fell to pieces. But they made the trip through weather that blistered the paint on the car, that froze radiators of parked cars, and climbed mountains that touched the clouds.

Orland Youths Return After Model T Journey

Orland—Two Orland youths are home again, returned from a 33 day tour of the United States In a 1919 model Ford. The youths, Kenneth and Charles Whitsett, purred into town in their ancient vehicle Friday night after traveling more than 6500 miles through a dozen states. The trip took them through Salt Lake City,

Buffalo, New York and Niagara Falls and back across the northern tip of the United States. While in Dearborn, Michigan,. the brothers were special guests of the Ford company plant. The vehicle, carrying a spare motor, made the trip with only minor difficulties. The trip was begun August 1st.

Whitsetts Complete Tour of Country In 1919 Ford

Charles and Kenneth Whitsett returned to their home here Friday after completing a 6500 mile tour of the United States in a 1919 Model T Ford roadster. High point of the trip was a visit to the Ford plant at Dearborn, Michigan, where they were honored at a dinner. The boys, sons of Mr. and Mrs. Willis Whitsett, left August 1st on the trip which took them as far east as Buffalo, N. Y., and to Windsor, Canada. En route they visited with relatives. They took the northern route back to Spokane, Washington, and on down to Orland. A spare engine was carried in addition to other spare parts in case of a breakdown, and it was necessary to install it. Very little tire or mechanical trouble was experienced. Officials at the Ford factory were impressed with the durability of the old machine and took photo-graphs for the publication in the company magazine.

Rural News
—Eastside
Mrs. L. M. Reager

Charles and Kenneth Whitsett left Friday on a trip east planning to go as far as Indiana if Kenneth's Model T Ford holds out that long.

Word comes from Kenneth and Charles Whitsett that they have succeeded in getting beyond Cheyenne Wyo., in their Model T Ford. They had a little trouble at Cheyenne when another car ran into the trailer in which they have their beds and provisions, but damage was very slight.

Charles and Kenneth Whitsett phoned their parents, Mr. and Mrs. Willis Whitsett, last night to say they and their Model T have succeeded in reaching Monticello, Indiana where they are visiting at the Robert Zootman home. They plan to go on from there into Michigan.

Printed in the United States
By Bookmasters